baseball

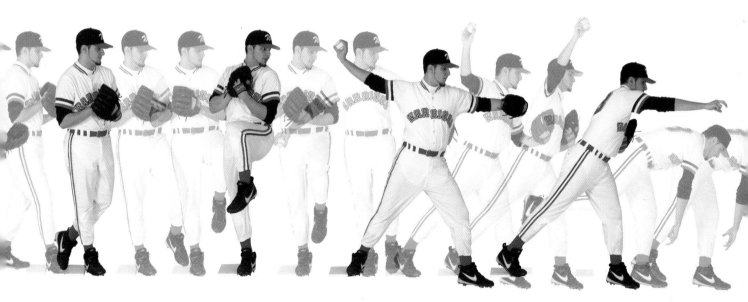

a *flow**motion*™ title

To: Taylor;

I hope you will enjoy this book
and feel better soon

From Teagan

baseball

alan smith & alan bloomfield

Sterling Publishing Co., Inc.

New York

Created and conceived by
Axis Publishing Limited
8c Accommodation Road
London NW11 8ED
www.axispublishing.co.uk

Creative Director: Siân Keogh
Managing Editor: Brian Burns
Project Designer: Juliet Brown
Project Editor: Madeleine Jennings
Production Manager: Sue Bayliss
Photographer: Mike Good

Library of Congress Cataloging-in-Publication
Data Available

10 9 8 7 6 5 4 3 2 1

Published in 2002 by Sterling Publishing Co., Inc.
387 Park Avenue South, New York, NY 10016
Text and images © Axis Publishing Limited 2002
Distributed in Canada by Sterling Publishing
C/o Canadian Manda Group,
One Atlantic Avenue, Suite 105
Toronto, Ontario, M6K 3E7, Canada

Separation by
United Graphics Pte Limited
Printed and bound by
Star Standard (Pte) Limited

Sterling ISBN 0–8069–9367–7

a *flowmotion*™ title

baseball

contents

introduction   **6**

the basics   **16**

pitching   **22**

catching   **36**

fielding   **46**

hitting   **72**

base running   **82**

index   **94**

understanding baseball

The game of baseball is often described as America's national pastime, but it is watched and played by millions of people in over 100 other countries throughout the world. Both boys and girls play baseball, although girls usually change to fast-pitch softball when they are older.

What is baseball?

Baseball is a bat-and-ball game played between two teams of nine players. There are nine innings in a game. In each inning both teams take a turn at batting (offense) and fielding (defense). The inning is over when three batters are put out. In the event of a tie at the end of the ninth inning, extra whole innings are played until the tie is broken and there is a winner.

Before the game, each team has to give the home plate umpire its line-up. This lists the starting players and their fielding positions in the order they will bat. If a player is taken out of the game at any time, he cannot return. The substitute must take the original player's place in the batting line-up, but is allowed to field in any position.

The aim of the game

The aim of the game is to score more runs than the opposing team. To score a run, the batter has to touch each base in turn and return to home plate. If he has hit the ball far enough, he can run around them all in one go—a home run. If not, he can be advanced one base at a time by the batters who bat after him. For a run to count, he must reach home plate safely before three of his team mates are out and the inning is over.

Balls and strikes

The strike zone is an imaginary area between the batter's knees and chest, directly over home plate.

A ball is a pitch thrown outside the strike zone that the batter does not swing at. If a batter receives four balls, he gets a free pass (a walk) to first base.

A strike is a pitch that:

- Passes through the strike zone without bouncing.
- The batter swings at and misses completely.
- The batter hits into foul territory when he has fewer than two strikes against him. (If the batter already has two strikes against him when he hits a foul ball, the count remains at two strikes.)

If a batter receives three strikes, he is out (struck out).

A batter ready to hit a strike (in red zone).

Fair or foul?

A fair ball is a batted ball that settles or is touched by a fielder in fair territory before first or third base, or lands in fair territory beyond first or third base, even if it then rolls over the foul line.

A foul ball is a batted ball that lands in foul territory and stays there, or that lands in fair territory and rolls over the foul line before it passes first or third base.

Safe or out?

A batter can get on base safely in a number of ways. For example:

- He receives four balls—a walk.
- He hits the ball in fair territory and reaches first base before the fielding team can get the ball there—a base hit or single.
- He is hit by a pitched ball.

There are a number of ways in which a batter can be out. For example:

- He has three strikes against him—a strike out.
- He hits the ball in the air and a fielder catches it—a fly out.
- He hits the ball on the ground and a fielder throws or carries it to first base before he can get there—a ground out.
- As a runner, he is touched by a fielder with the ball, or with the fielder's glove containing the ball, while he is not in contact with a base—a tag out.

WHO IS INVOLVED IN THE GAME

In addition to the players, there are four other groups of people involved in the game:

- **managers:** Each team has a manager who usually sits in the dugout giving the coaches instructions to pass on to the players
- **coaches:** The batting team has one coach at first base and another at third base. They use sign language to instruct the players and tell runners when to stop, keep running, or slide.
- **scorers:** Each game has an official scorer who sits outside the field of play. His job is to score the game accurately, compile the official score sheet, and produce statistics.
- **umpires:** A team of umpires on the field controls the game. **the plate umpire** stands behind the catcher at home plate. He controls the whole game, and one of his main jobs is to decide whether pitches are balls or strikes. He wears protective clothing so that he isn't injured if the ball hits him.
the base umpires stand near the bases and make decisions about plays around the bases and in the outfield. They also decide whether balls hit into the outfield are fair or foul and if a ball has cleared the fence for a home run.

field of play

Baseball is played on an enclosed field formed by two lines (called foul lines) and a fence. These lines start at home plate and run through first and third bases to the outfield fence to create a 90-degree arc. The area inside the foul lines and the fence is called fair territory, and the areas outside are called foul territory. Behind home plate there is a netting backstop to protect spectators.

The distance between home plate and the backstop varies, but in senior baseball it should be at least 60ft (18m). The height and width can vary, but it must be big enough to prevent the ball from flying past the batter and into the crowd.

The inner part of fair territory is called the infield, and is usually partly covered with dirt. It is made up of home plate and first, second, and third bases, laid out in a square (the diamond). Home plate is a five-sided piece of hard white rubber set into the ground. The bases are square pieces of white canvas filled with foam, anchored to the ground. The distance between these bases varies depending on the players' ages, but in senior baseball they are 90ft (27.43m) apart.

On each side of home plate is a batter's box. The batter must be standing in one of these boxes when he hits the ball or he will be called out. Behind home plate is a catcher's box, where the catcher fields the ball. The catcher must stay in this box until the pitcher has released the ball.

The pitcher's mound is the raised area that the pitcher stands on when he is pitching. On top of the mound is the pitcher's plate (or rubber) which is a rectangle of hard white rubber set into the ground. The distance from the front of the rubber to the back of home plate in senior baseball is 60ft 6in (18.44m). The outer part of fair territory, beyond the bases, is called the outfield and is usually covered with grass.

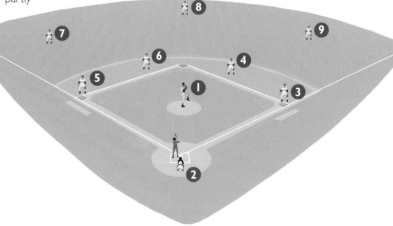

1. Pitcher
2. Catcher
3. First baseman
4. Second baseman
5. Third baseman
6. Shortstop
7. Left fielder
8. Center fielder
9. Right fielder

Equipment

The two main pieces of equipment are the bat and ball. Players also use gloves (mitts) and other protective equipment. Professionals use wooden bats, but most amateurs use hard-wearing aluminum bats. Balls have a core of cork or rubber bound with yarn and are covered with white leather.

All fielders wear a leather glove with a pocket to make it easier to catch the ball. Infielders prefer smaller gloves so they can transfer the ball from the pocket to the throwing hand more quickly. Outfielders prefer larger gloves with deeper pockets for catching fly balls. The catcher wears a special catcher's mitt, which is larger than an infielder's, with more padding. The first baseman also has a special mitt with a large pocket and more padding to make catching balls easier and less painful. Batters often wear leather batting gloves for a better grip. A batter must wear a helmet, usually made of plastic with foam padding, whenever he is batting or base running. Catchers wear special protective equipment (see page 12).

Warming up

It is very important to warm up properly before every practice or game. This helps you to prepare both mentally and physically and can help to avoid injury. Your warmup routine should involve a short run followed by a series of stretches to loosen up your muscles. Always stretch in a slow, controlled way, and avoid bouncing or any sudden movements.

Safety

Baseball can be a dangerous game, and it is therefore vital that players follow safety precautions at all times. In addition to wearing the safety equipment mentioned above, there are three other important points:

- Remove all jewelry before starting any physical exercise.
- Always be aware of what is going on around you and NEVER turn your back on the ball.
- All boys must wear a protective cup held in place by a jock strap or athletic supporter at all times.

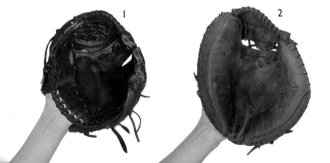

BASEBALL GLOVES/MITTS

1. Infielder's glove; note the small pocket.

2. Catcher's mitt with extra thick padding.

3. First baseman's mitt with wider pocket and extra padding.

playing the game

Pitching

A good pitcher can have more influence on a game than a good hitter. A smart pitcher who mixes his pitches and is able to throw them all accurately will be more successful than one who relies on speed alone. This is known as control, and is the pitcher's best weapon.

The pitcher's main job is to stop the batter from getting on base. If he pitches the ball differently each time, the batter will not know what to expect and will find it harder to hit the ball solidly.

The two most important pitches are the fastball and change-up. These can be thrown by any pitcher, but must be thrown accurately to be effective.

As pitchers get older, and their arms get stronger, they can throw breaking pitches. By using a different grip, they can make the ball spin and move in the air, making it more difficult to hit.

There are two legal pitching positions, which are called the windup and the set position (or stretch). Although either position can be used at any time, they are normally used as follows:

- The windup gives more power and control, and is used when a stolen base is not a threat, so the pitcher can afford the extra time it takes to deliver the ball to the plate.
- The set position is used when there are runners on base and the pitcher wants to stop them from stealing. He can throw to the plate or any base occupied by a runner.

The pitcher can throw the ball as hard as he likes, but never at a batter, as this could result in the pitcher being ejected from the game. Once he has pitched, the pitcher becomes the fifth infielder and must field any ball hit near him.

HERE ARE THREE WAYS TO MIX PITCHES

- **speed:** pitch the ball at different speeds. The batter will find it difficult to adjust his swing to hit a fastball if he is expecting a slower delivery, and a fastball will look even faster if it is thrown after a slower pitch (change-up).
- **location:** aim at different areas of the strike zone. The batter will have trouble hitting a ball at chest level if he is expecting a pitch at his knees, or if it is inside when he is expecting it outside.
- **trajectory:** pitch the ball from different ends of the rubber and/or with a higher or lower arm action. This will change the trajectory of the ball as it travels toward the batter and will make it more difficult to hit.

Hitting

Hitting requires good hand/eye coordination. Even the best major-league batters only manage to hit the ball safely in 3 out of every 10 attempts. The batter's main job is to get on base and attempt to score a run. His success depends on both his mental and physical skills.

At the plate, the batter should be confident of a hit. He should know the strike zone and be prepared to adjust his style to protect it, especially when he has two strikes. He should leave pitches that give him trouble and have the patience to wait for one he knows he can hit. He should always be ready to hit. A good

For a proper grip, keep the fingers slightly loose

principle is to think every pitch is a fastball strike until proven otherwise.

The batter should choose a bat he feels comfortable with. Many players use a bat that is too heavy. As bat speed is more important than strength, it is better to use a lighter bat that is easier to control.

Good hitting is almost impossible without a comfortable grip. The bat should be held mainly in the fingers so the hands and wrists can move freely. It should not be held too tightly because this will tense the forearm muscles and make it difficult to swing smoothly.

The stance should be comfortable, and the batter should be able to reach any ball in the strike zone. His bat and his entire body should be perfectly still and balanced as he waits for the pitcher to start his delivery.

Many players swing too hard and affect their timing. A moderately hard swing with a strong wrist action is more effective. During his swing, the batter should keep his head still and never take his eyes off the ball. There are situations that call for specialized hitting. For example:

BUNT: a gentle tap into the infield to try to get on base and/or advance a runner.

HIT AND RUN: as the runner from first base starts running toward second base, the batter hits a ground ball to try to advance the runner beyond second base to third base or even home plate.

SACRIFICE FLY: a fly ball hit deep into the outfield enables a runner on third base to try to score a run once the ball has been caught.

SQUEEZE: a sacrifice bunt to allow a runner on third base to attempt to score a run.

Catching

The catcher has a very important role on the team. From his position behind home plate, he is the only fielder who has a complete view of the defense. Because of this, on top of his normal playing duties, he has to be team leader and direct defensive plays during the game.

The catcher plays a varied and crucial role that calls for a number of skills. Note his protective equipment.

AFTER CALLING AND RECEIVING PITCHES, THE CATCHER'S MAIN JOB IS TO SUPPORT THE PITCHER AND HELP MAKE HIM MORE EFFECTIVE. TO DO THIS HE WILL:

- know the strengths and weaknesses of the batters and call pitches that will be most effective against them.
- use hidden hand signals to tell the pitcher the type and location of the pitch to throw.
- position the fielders depending on the game situation and the batter at the plate.

THE CATCHER IS ALSO RESPONSIBLE FOR FIELDING AT HOME PLATE. HE MUST BE ABLE TO:

- **block wild pitches:** stop the pitched ball from getting past him and so prevent runners from advancing.
- **throw out runners:** catch a pitched ball and throw it to any base that a runner is stealing to try to get him tagged out.
- **block home plate:** catch a thrown ball from another fielder and tag the runner to stop him from scoring.
- **catch pop-ups:** catch a ball hit in the air around home plate that other fielders cannot reach.

Fielding

The defensive team's job is to field the ball and stop runners from advancing around the bases and scoring runs. Each fielder should know what to do with the ball when it is hit to him. He should always be aware of the score, the inning, the number and location of runners, the number of outs, and the count on the batter.

There are nine fielding positions in baseball, six in the infield and three in the outfield. Although each position needs some special skills, all fielders must be able to catch the ball, keep it in front of them when fielding, and throw the ball accurately.

In addition to the pitcher and catcher, there are four other infielders; first base, second base, shortstop, and third base. They defend the areas around the bases, tag runners, and relay throws from the outfielders. Infielders need to be agile and have good range and quick reflexes.

The three outfielders are left fielder, center fielder, and right fielder. They have to defend the whole of the outfield and back up the bases. Because of the size of the area they have to cover, outfielders need to be fast runners and have strong throwing arms.

Fielders can put opposing team players out by catching the ball in the air, tagging them, or forcing them out on the bases. Sometimes, two outs are made on one hit ball—a double play. Double plays are most often made when two players are forced out at successive bases. Another common double play happens when a runner fails to return to the base he was occupying before a caught ball has been thrown to that base.

Base running

Base running is another very important part of the game. As soon as the batter puts the ball in play, he becomes a base runner and he must try to reach first base safely. His job then is to try to advance around the other bases and cross home plate to score a run before the third out is made.

There are a number of ways in which he can then progress around the diamond:

FORCED: on a batted fair ball, the batter must run to first base. A runner already on first base is therefore forced to run to second base. If there are runners on first and second bases or if the bases are loaded with runners occupying all three bases, all runners are forced to run to the next base.

UNFORCED: if a runner is on second base when first base is unoccupied, he is not forced to run on a base hit, or a walk. However, if the ball is hit in fair territory or a pitch gets away from the catcher, the runner can run to third base or further at his own risk.

STEALING: the runner can attempt to run to the next base even when the ball has not been hit. He would normally do this as the pitcher is delivering a pitch to the plate by taking a few steps off the base he is occupying (leading off) and then running to the next base. To be safe, he must reach the base before the ball arrives; otherwise, he may be tagged out.

TAGGING-UP: if a batted ball is caught in fair or foul territory, a runner must first retouch the base he is occupying (tag-up) before he is allowed to advance to another base.

SLIDING: runners are not allowed to over-run second and third bases. To stop at a base and to avoid being tagged out, a runner can decide to slide into a base. Here are several different types of slide, for example:

- Feet first: this is the basic slide and is the safest.
- Head first: sliding head first takes less time, but is potentially more dangerous and should not be attempted by younger players.
- Hook: this is used to slide around the fielder to avoid a tag
- Pop-up: this is used to pop-up into a standing position as you arrive at a base.

NB: FOUL BALLS: a runner is not allowed to advance on a foul ball unless it is caught (see tagging-up, above).

go with the flow

The special *Flowmotion* images used in this book have been created to make sure that you see the whole of each move—not just selected highlights. The captions along the bottom of the images provide additional information to help you execute each move confidently. Below this, another layer of information iindicates key moments for holding a position, preparing to throw, preparing to catch, releasing the ball, etc. The highlighted illustratrations in the spreads show key positions of each action. Note the direction each player is facing, the position of his feet and hands, and especially the way he is holding his glove or bat. The sequences clearly show the fluidity of movement crucial to success in playing baseball.

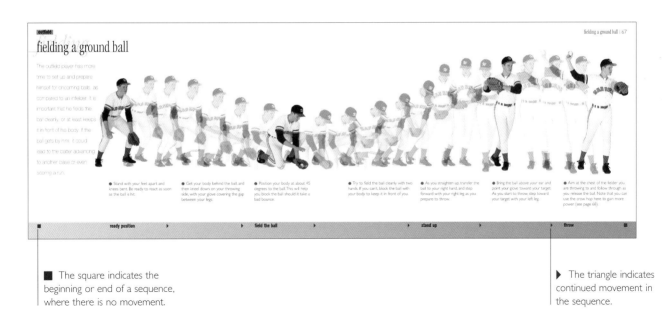

outfield
fielding a ground ball

fielding a ground ball | 67

The outfield player has more time to set up and prepare himself for oncoming balls, as compared to an infielder. It is important that he fields the ball cleanly, or at least keeps it in front of his body. If the ball gets by him, it could lead to the batter advancing to another base or even scoring a run.

● Stand with your feet apart and knees bent. Be ready to react as soon as the ball is hit.

● Get your body behind the ball, and then kneel down on your throwing side, with your glove covering the gap between your legs.

● Position your body at about 45 degrees to the ball. This will help you block the ball should it take a bad bounce.

● Try to field the ball cleanly with two hands. If you can't, block the ball with your body to keep it in front of you.

● As you straighten up, transfer the ball to your right hand, and step forward with your right leg as you prepare to throw.

● Bring the ball above your ear and point your glove toward your target. As you start to throw, step toward your target with your left leg.

● Aim at the chest of the fielder you are throwing to and follow through as you release the ball. Note that you can use the crow hop here to gain more power (see page 68).

■   ready position ▶   field the ball ▶   stand up ▶   throw ■

■ The square indicates the beginning or end of a sequence, where there is no movement.

▶ The triangle indicates continued movement in the sequence.

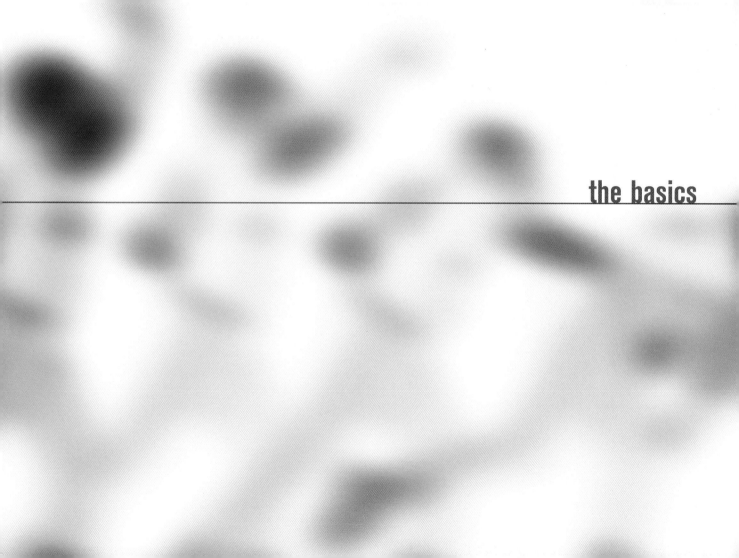

the basics

throwing *the basics*

Each baseball position needs special skills, but all players must be able to throw the ball strongly and accurately. You need a strong throwing arm, but holding the ball correctly, using your whole body in the throwing motion, and following through fully, will help you make stronger and more accurate throws.

● Grip the ball with your index and middle fingers across the wide seams at the top and your thumb on the bottom. Step your right foot out in front of you at a 45-degree angle.

● Turn your body to the right as you transfer you weight onto your right foot. Pick up your left foot and prepare to step toward your target.

● Raise your glove to chest height as you bring your left foot forward. Take your right arm back and above your ear as you begin to step.

● Transfer your weight onto your left leg as you step toward your target. Keep your right arm up so the ball is well above your ear.

● Aim the ball at the chest of the fielder you are throwing the ball to. As you throw, push off your right foot to gain momentum.

● As you release the ball, flick your wrist forward and downward to add more power to your throw. The point at which you release it defines the path the ball will take.

● Follow through by allowing your body to bend forward, bringing your right arm down toward your left knee.

prepare to throw ▶ ▶ **release the ball** ▶ **follow through** ◼

catching

the basics

Always keep your eye on the ball and try to catch it using both hands whenever possible. Position yourself so the ball arrives at the center of your body. Allow your hands to "give" a little as you catch the ball.

● Stand with your feet shoulder width apart and knees slightly bent. Keep your hands out in front of you, with elbows bent.

● You should aim to catch the ball at the center of your body. So, depending on where the ball is, step to either side in order to move your body behind the ball.

● Reach out with your glove toward the ball. Catch the ball in the glove and close your bare hand around it to secure the ball. Bend your elbows to bring your hands into your chest to absorb the impact of the ball.

● Bring the glove and ball back toward your chest as you simultaneously remove the ball with your right hand.

● Transfer your weight to your right leg. As you step with your left leg and prepare to throw, raise your right arm behind you so the ball is behind your ear.

● Shift your weight forward onto your left leg as you bring your right arm up above your ear.

● Push off your right foot as you step into the throw. Bring your right arm through, flicking your wrist as you release the ball.

transfer ball to throwing hand ▶ **prepare to throw** ▶ **throw the ball** ◼

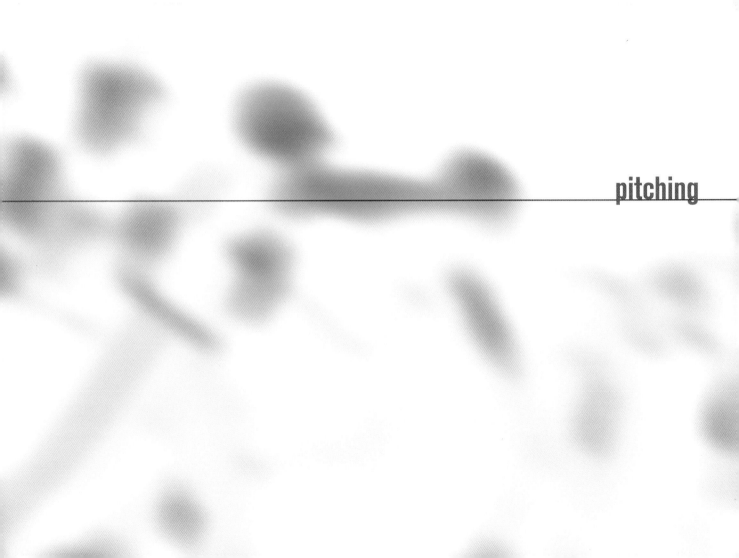

pitching

windup—right hand

The aim of a pitcher is to prevent the batter from getting to first base. Pitching from the windup is a great way to do this because it means you throw harder. However, the most important aspect of any pitch is location, known as "hitting the spot."

● Stand with both feet on the rubber facing home plate to take the sign from the catcher. Hide the ball from the batter's view so he cannot see the type of grip you are using.

● Step back off the rubber with your left foot. Pivot your right foot through 90 degrees, placing it in contact with the front of the rubber. Bring your right hand holding the ball into the glove. Raise both hands to your chest.

● Keep your eye on the target as you raise your left knee up to waist height. Turn your body so your left buttock is facing toward the batter.

● As you begin to separate your hands, bring your left leg down and forward. Keep your back straight to maintain balance. The ball should be above ear level, facing away from the batter with your glove facing down.

● Land on the ball of your left foot and swivel your hips as you open your body. Tuck your glove into your chest as you push off the rubber with your right foot and throw the ball.

● Lift your right foot off the rubber and allow your body to follow through with the momentum of the pitch, bending your back as you do so. Bring your right arm down toward your left foot.

● Allow your right leg to follow through to land beside your left. At the same time, turn your body to face the batter and bring both hands foward so that you are in a balanced position, ready to field the ball.

windup—left hand

Remember that you would normally only pitch from the windup when there are no runners on base, as you can afford the extra time it takes to deliver the ball to the plate. Remember also to shield the ball from the batter's view so he cannot see your grip and guess the type of pitch you are planning to throw.

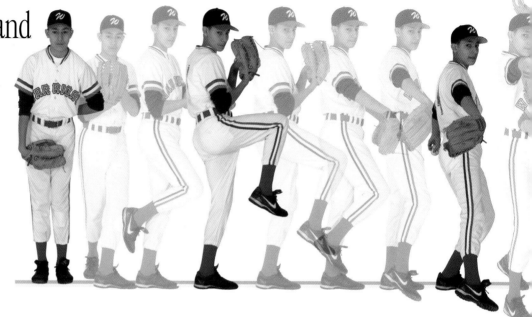

● Put both feet on the rubber facing home plate to take the sign from the catcher. Step back off the rubber with your right foot. Pivot your left foot through 90 degrees, placing it in contact with the front of the rubber.

● Bring your left hand holding the ball into the glove. Raise both hands to your chest. Watch the target and raise your right knee to waist height. Turn your body so your right buttock is facing toward the batter.

● As you begin to separate your hands, bring your right leg down and forward. Keep your back straight to maintain your balance. The ball should be above ear level, facing away from the batter, and your glove facing down.

● Land on the ball of your right foot and swivel your hips as you open your body. Tuck your glove into your chest as you push off the rubber with your left foot and throw the ball.

● Lift your left foot off the rubber and allow your body to follow through with the momentum of the throw, bending your back as you do so.

● Keep moving forward and downward so that your left arm comes down outside your right foot. Allow your left leg to follow through and land beside your right.

● At the same time turn your body to face the batter and bring both hands forward so you are in a balanced position, ready to field the ball.

release the ball　▶　**follow through**　▶　　　　▶　**adopt a fielding position**　■

set position—right hand

When there are runners on base, a pitcher needs to use the set position to try to prevent runners from stealing. In the set position you must come to a complete stop. You must not move your shoulders or any other part of your body to try to see the runner. You are only allowed to move your head.

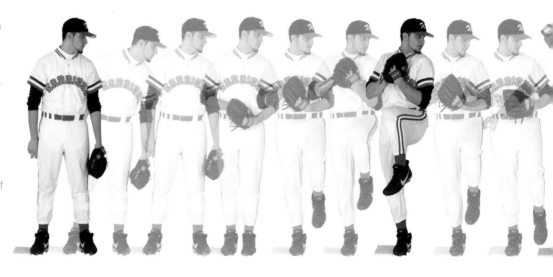

● You must have your right foot in contact with the rubber and your hands apart as you take the sign from the catcher.

● Bring your hands together and hold them in a relaxed position around belt height. This is the set position in which you must come to a complete stop.

● Keep your eye on the target as you raise your left knee up to waist height. Turn your body slightly so your left buttock is facing toward the batter.

● As you begin to separate your hands, bring your left leg down and forward. Keep your back straight to maintain your balance. The ball should be above ear level, facing away from the batter, and your glove facing down.

● Land on the ball of your left foot and swivel your hips as you open your body. Tuck your glove into your chest as you push off the rubber with your right foot and throw the ball.

● Lift your right foot off the rubber and allow your body to follow through with the momentum of the pitch, bending your back as you do so. Bring your right arm down toward your left foot.

● Allow your right leg to follow through to land beside your left. At the same time, turn your body to face the batter and bring both hands foward so you are in a balanced position, ready to field the ball.

▶   release the ball   ▶   ▶   adopt a fielding position   ■

set position—left hand

Holding runners at first base is much easier for a left-hander than it is for a right-hander because he is facing the runner and can see what is going on. Remember, you must have your left foot in contact with the rubber and your hands apart as you take the sign from the catcher.

● Bring your hands together and hold them in a relaxed position around belt height. This is the set position in which you must come to a complete stop.

● Keep your eye on the target as you raise your right knee up to waist height. Turn your body so your right buttock is facing toward the batter.

● As you begin to separate your hands, bring your right leg down and forward. Keep your back straight to maintain your balance. The ball should be above ear level, facing away from the batter, and your glove facing down.

● Land on the ball of your right foot and swivel your hips as you open your body. Tuck your glove into your chest as you push off the rubber with your left foot and throw the ball.

● Lift your left foot off the rubber and allow your body to follow through with the momentum of the throw, bending your back as you do so.

● Keep moving forward and downward so that your left arm comes down outside your right foot. Allow your left leg to follow through and land beside your right.

● At the same time, turn your body to face the batter and bring both hands forward so you are in a balanced position, ready to field the ball.

release the ball   ▶   **follow through**   ▶   **adopt a fielding position**   ■

pick-off to first base—right hand

A pick-off play is where a pitcher throws the ball to a base hoping to catch the runner off the base, to be tagged out. This is done by stepping off the rubber (see here) or directly from the rubber (see pages 34-35). It is hard for a right-handed pitcher to attempt a pick off as he is facing away from first base.

● You may either be given a sign by the catcher to attempt a pick-off at first base or you may decide to do so on your own.

● Remember, you must come to a complete stop in the set position. Remember also that you are only allowed to move your head to look at the runner.

● From the set position, step back off the rubber with your right foot. At the same time, begin to part your hands.

● Step directly toward first base with your left foot, and begin to turn your body to face the runner.

● Since the pick-off to first base is a surprise throw, speed is essential so you should make this turn quickly.

● Then pivot on your right foot as you raise your right arm and begin to throw the ball.

● Tuck your glove into your body as you throw the ball. This is a short throw using a snap of the wrist. Remember that because you have stepped off the rubber, you do *not* have to throw the ball.

step towards first base ▶ ▶ **pivot and throw the ball** ▶ ■

pick-off to first base—left hand

A pick-off to first base is easier for a left-hander because he does not have to turn his body to throw the ball. Using the method shown here, the pitcher always has his foot in contact with the rubber so if he steps toward first base he *must* throw the ball there.

● You should try to give the impression that you are about to pitch to the batter.

● Stand side on with your left foot touching the rubber. As you bring your hands up toward your chest, lift your right foot.

● Raise your right knee to around waist height as if you were going to pitch the ball to the batter.

● Continue as you would for a normal pitch. Look toward the plate as you separate your hands and prepare to throw the ball.

● Instead of stepping toward home plate, step toward first base. Turn your head toward your target at the last second and throw the ball to the first baseman.

● Since this is a surprise tactic, speed is essential. You must throw the ball quickly, directly at the first baseman's mitt.

● Remember, on this pick-off move where you have not stepped off the rubber, you *must* throw the ball to first base or a balk will be called.

▶ **step towards first base** ▶ **release the ball** ▶ ■

catching

blocking wild pitches

When there are runners on base, it is important that the catcher blocks any wild pitches to prevent the runners from advancing. The idea is not to try to catch the ball, but to knock it down in front of you, off your chest protector.

● Keep your throwing hand behind your glove. Make sure your fingers are loosely curled—this will help to prevent injury if they get hit by the ball.

● This is the receiving position with runners on base. Your backside should be slightly raised to allow you to move to either side to block a wild pitch or to throw the ball.

● On a ball pitched to your left-hand side, lean toward your left as you begin to drop down onto your left knee and extend your right leg.

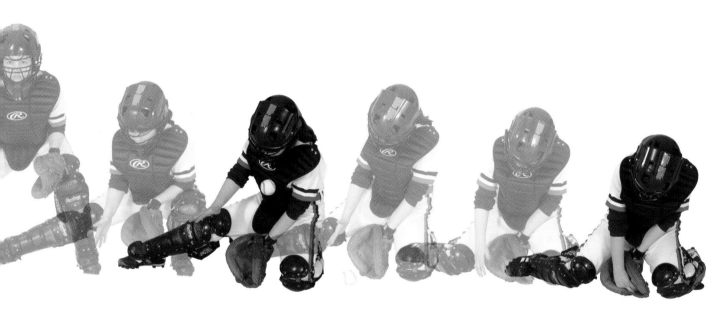

● Turn your body toward the direction of the oncoming ball, so you can block it square on.

● Position your glove so it is in the gap between your legs. Your upper body should lean into the ball to help knock the ball down. Keep your chin tucked into your chest to prevent the ball from hitting your throat.

● Once you have knocked the ball down, quickly scoop it up into the pocket of your glove with your bare hand. When you are sure the ball is safely in the glove, look up to see if you need to make a play.

● Note—if a ball is pitched to your right-hand side, follow the same procedure but substitute the word "right" in place of the word "left."

drop down ▶ **knock ball down** ▶ **pick ball up** ▶ ■

throwing to second base

When there is a runner on first base, the pressure is on the catcher to make a quick throw to second base to try to get the runner out if he tries to steal. Remember, as there are runners on base, you must keep your throwing hand behind the glove, ready to make a quick throw.

● Position the toe of your right foot roughly in line with with the heel of your left foot. This will enable you to move quickly into a throwing position if necessary.

● Catch the ball and take a short step with your right foot and turn your left shoulder toward second base.

● As you step, bring the glove and ball up to your right ear as quickly as possible.

■   **squat down low** ▶   ▶ **ready to throw** ▶

● Step forward with your left foot as you prepare to throw to second base. Remember, this has to be a quick throw if you are to stop the runner from stealing.

● Make the throw short and sharp. The power for this throw comes from your shoulder and wrist.

● Aim the throw slightly toward the first-base side of second base to make it easier for the fielder to tag the runner.

● Follow through by bringing your right arm down toward your left side. Try to make the throw as flat as possible to get the ball to second base quickly.

▶ **release the ball**　　　▶ **snap wrist**　　　▶ **follow through**

blocking home plate

The aim of this play is to stop runners from sliding directly into home plate. The catcher should position herself in front of the plate, forcing a runner to slide around her. Note it is illegal to block the plate, unless you are holding the ball and, at junior level, a runner cannot run into the catcher on purpose.

● Squat down with your backside slightly lifted so you can move in either direction to catch the ball.

● Put your throwing hand behind the catcher's glove, curling your fingers loosely for safety.

● Once the ball has been hit into play, remove your mask so you can see what is happening. Throw your mask to one side so it will not interfere with the play.

▶ **remove mask**　　▶ **discard your mask**　　▶

● If a runner is trying to get to home plate, position yourself about one or two feet up the third baseline in front of the plate. Face the fielder and prepare to receive the throw.

● Place your left foot, pointing toward third base, roughly on the base line. If a runner slides into your left leg, his foot will hit your leg-guard and your knee will flex naturally, avoiding injury.

● Once you catch the ball, turn your body so you are facing the runner. Hold the ball in your bare hand inside the glove.

● The reason you stand in this position is so the runner can only see a corner of the plate and must slide around you to score.

face towards the throw ▶ catch the ball ▶ face the runner ▶ prepare for tag ■

catching pop-ups

When a ball is hit directly up into the air, it is called a pop-up. You should remove your mask as quickly as possible so you can locate the ball and try to catch it. Remember, a foul ball—when caught—is still live, and any baserunners may attempt to advance.

● If there are no runners on base and there is no need for a quick throw, keep your throwing hand behind your back to protect it from being hit.

● Once the pop-up occurs, remove your mask as quickly as possible, and look to see where the ball is and start to move toward it.

● Discard your mask in the opposite direction to which you are moving so you don't trip over it.

● Always catch the ball with your back toward the infield because the spin of the ball will carry it in this direction.

● Put both hands out in front of you above head height in preparation for the catch. Remember, the spin will bring the ball toward you.

● Make sure your glove is open, facing upward, because the ball will be coming almost directly straight down. Take the ball with your extended glove hand and close your throwing hand around it.

● Remember, once you have caught the ball it is live, so turn to face the infield in case you need to make another play.

back facing infield ▶ **glove face up** ▶ **look for next play** ◼

fielding

fielding a ground ball

To field well, you need to be aggressive. You should not wait for the ball to come to you, but should move toward it, staying as low as possible and positioning yourself behind the ball.

● Keep your feet wide apart, knees bent, backside down, and body low to the ground. The toe of your right foot should be roughly in line with the heel of your left foot. The back of your glove should be touching the ground.

● Put your hands out in front of you in preparation for the oncoming ball. Your right hand should be just above the glove.

● Keep your eye on the ball all the way into your glove, and use your right hand to trap the ball once it is in the pocket of your glove.

● In this position, other fielders should be able to see the button on top of your cap as you field the ball.

■ **start low** ▶ **watch ball into the glove** ▶ ▶

● Make sure your hands are "soft," so when they receive the ball they give a little and you can bring the ball toward your abdomen.

● Once you have the ball, take a short step with your right foot as you transfer the ball to your throwing hand and turn your left shoulder toward your target.

● Bring your throwing arm back behind your ear as you prepare to throw. Snap your wrist as you release the ball, and make sure you follow through.

● Remember to try to make the whole play in one smooth, fluid movement resulting in a quick and accurate throw.

backhanding a ball

When a batter hits the ball to your right side, your first move should be a crossover step to the right. To do this, pivot on your right foot, turning your toes 90 degrees, and bring your left foot across so that your body also turns 90 degrees to the right-hand side.

● Just as you did for fielding a ground ball, start with your body low to the ground and your feet apart.

● Keeping your body low, pivot on the ball of your right foot as you start to turn your body toward your right. As you reach out for the ball, bring your left foot across your body.

● Bend your right leg, bringing your knee all the way to the ground if necessary. Extend your left arm so that your glove is out in front of the toes of your left foot.

● The top of your glove should be touching the ground and your forearm as vertical as possible. Your glove face should be open and facing the ball.

● By starting with your glove low, you can come up with the ball if it bounces higher than expected.

● After catching the ball, take a short step, with your right foot behind your left, and start to straighten up.

● As you come up, transfer the ball into your right hand, and brace yourself on your right foot to stop your momentum.

● As you straighten, turn your left shoulder toward your target. Take your right arm back behind your ear; step, and throw.

going to your left

When a batter hits a ball to your left side, you should make a crossover step with your right foot, pivoting on your left foot. Ideally, you should always try to get behind the ball. When this is not possible because the ball is too far out of reach, you will need to adopt this technique.

● With your feet apart and your knees bent, squat down low to the ground in preparation to field the ball, hands out in front.

● Keeping your body low, pivot on your left foot as you bring your right foot across your body.

● Make sure you keep your knees bent and your glove low and in line with your feet.

● As you field the ball, bring your right hand onto the ball, watching the ball all the way into the glove.

● Allow your hands to "give" as you field the ball, and bring your hands up into the center of your body as you step with your left foot.

● Take a short step onto your right foot as you straighten up and transfer the ball to your right hand.

● Turn your left shoulder toward your target, and bring your right hand above and behind your ear.

● Keep your eyes on your target as you step toward him, and throw the ball. Remember to aim at his chest.

▶ **step onto your right foot**   **prepare to throw**   ▶ **release the ball**   ■

fielding
tagging runners

The aim of this play is to try to tag the runner with the ball before he gets to his intended base. Once you have tagged your runner, look up to see if there is a possibility of another play.

● Stand at the front of the base or straddle it. Keep your knees slightly bent as you face toward the throw.

● Try not to reach for the ball; let it come to you. When you catch it, move your glove directly to the base as quickly as possible.

● The easiest way to tag the runner out is to place your glove, with the ball inside, at the front edge of the base. As the runner slides, he will contact your glove, effectively tagging himself out.

▶ **catch ball** ▶ **tag runner** ▶

● Always try to tag the runner with the back of the glove. This should stop the ball from being dislodged.

● Once the runner has been tagged out, straighten up and transfer the ball to your right hand.

● Readjust your weight, and look around you to see if there is a possibility of another play.

● Remember, you are not tied to the base. If the throw is off target, go and get it.

▶   ▶   **prepare for next play**   ▶   ■

first baseman stretch

The idea behind stretching for the ball is to receive it sooner. The fraction of a second this saves could mean the difference between the runner being out or safe.

● When the ball is hit to another fielder, you should try to get to first base as quickly as possible.

● You should be aware of the position of the base beforehand so you don't need to look at it when you are running toward it.

● Locate the base and place your foot on the inside corner of the base (right-hander, right foot; left-hander, left foot). This will prevent you from being hit by the runner, who should run to the outside part of the base.

● Stand with your feet shoulder width apart, and hold up your glove to give a target to the infielder. Be ready to move to your left or right to catch the ball if the throw is inaccurate.

● As the ball comes toward you, step in the direction of the throw, extending your forward leg out as far as you can while maintaining your balance.

● Make sure your glove hand is fully extended. It may help to keep your other hand behind your back to maintain balance.

● Once you have caught the ball, take your foot off the base to avoid being hit by the runner.

fielding
double play—feed

A double play combination is the key to any good defensive team. The intention is to get two people out in a single play. This play is normally used at second base. Getting the first runner out is most important, so a good feed is essential.

● Start with your body low and balanced, with your feet apart and your hands out in front as you field the ball.

● Once the ball is in the pocket of your glove, use your other hand to trap it to prevent it from rolling out.

● Once you have fielded the ball, turn your body to face the person you are going to throw it to and grip the ball in your bare hand.

● Move your glove away to show him the ball. This will help him to follow it as you toss it to him.

● Stretch your arm forward, and move your body in the direction of your target as you begin to throw the ball.

● As you pass the ball with a short toss, step toward your target, keeping your wrist and forearm stiff.

● Follow through with the toss. Extending your arm allows your body to continue moving in the direction of the throw. This will ensure a smooth release and an accurate toss.

show the ball ▶ **keep wrist stiff** ▶ **follow the ball** ■

fielding double play pivot—shortstop

This is slightly easier than the second base double play (see pages 62–63) because you are already moving toward your target. For this play to be successful, you need to be quick, both with your feet and your hands. Try not to rush, however, as this may cause a bad throw.

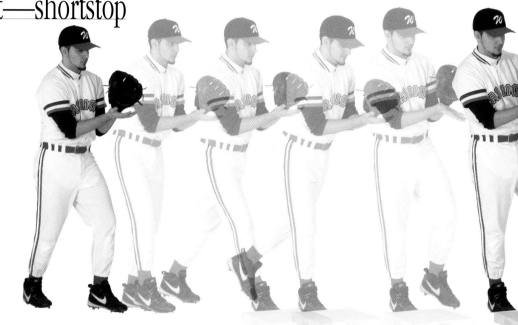

● In order to receive his throw, move quickly toward second base, making a straight line between yourself, second base, and the second baseman.

● As you approach second base, slow down and bring yourself under control by using short "stutter" steps, ready to move in any direction if the throw is inaccurate.

● Use your glove to give the second baseman a target . Keep your right hand next to your glove; this allows you to catch with both hands and make a quick transfer.

● Place your right foot by the outside corner of the base and your left foot toward right field. As you catch the ball, do not close the glove, but trap the ball with your right hand.

● Jump from your left foot to your right foot toward right field, clipping the outside corner of the base with your right toe. This step should carry you out of the way of the runner.

● As you jump to your right foot, square your shoulders toward first base and transfer the ball to your right hand. After you land on your right foot, step toward first base with your left foot.

● Complete the play with a short "snap" throw to first base. The key to this play is to execute it in one single, fluid motion. You will need quick hands and quick feet.

catch the ball   ▶   **clip second base**   ▶   **throw to first base**   ■

fielding

double play pivot—second baseman

There are a number of ways to execute this play, and players should experiment to find which one suits them best. The double play pivot shown here avoids the runner, so it is one of the safest.

● Get to second base as quickly as possible, then bring yourself under control using short "stutter" steps.

● Place your left foot on the outside corner of the base and face towards third base. Don't put it on the top; otherwise, you may slip. Use your glove as a target, keeping your throwing hand next to your glove.

● Do not close the glove, but trap the ball in the pocket with your throwing hand. This will enable a quick transfer of the ball.

▶ **give target** ▶ **catch the ball** ▶

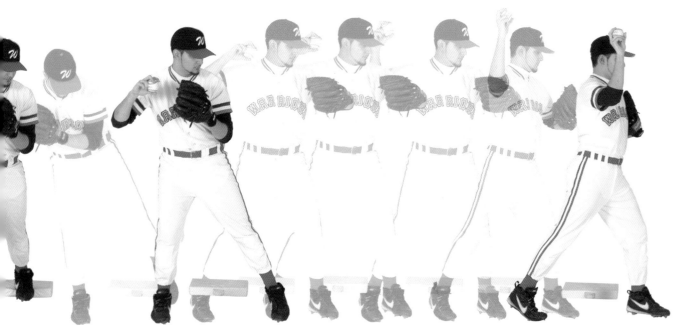

● As you catch the ball, jump onto your right foot toward third base, taking you out of the path of the runner. As you jump, transfer the ball to your right hand.

● Brace yourself on your right foot to stop your body's momentum, and pick up the target offered by the first baseman.

● Bring your arm up, ready to throw. Keep your eye on the target as you step your left leg toward first base.

● Make the throw to first base short and hard, with a snap of your wrist and forearm. Remember, you need quick hands and quick feet.

avoid runner ▶ locate target ▶ throw the ball to first base ■

infield
relay *fielding*

The reason for making a relay throw is to ensure a quicker, more accurate throw than the alternative, single looping throw from one fielder to another.

● Stand with your feet apart, and hold your hands high in the air to give the outfielder a target.

● As the throw comes in, try to read the path of the ball, and position yourself to catch the ball on your glove side.

● As you prepare to catch the ball, turn your body sideways. This will allow a quick transfer. Do not close the glove, but trap the ball in it with your right hand.

● Catch the ball with your weight on your left foot, and bring your right foot up to your left as you transfer the ball to your throwing hand.

● Step toward your target with your left foot as you separate your hands, ready to throw the ball.

● Bring your throwing arm back as you prepare to make the throw to the next fielder, and push off your right foot to gain momentum.

● Try to make the whole play as fluid as possible. Your body should continue to move in the direction of the throw, which will help make the relay faster and more accurate.

catch and transfer ▶ ▶ **throw** ▶ ■

fielding a ground ball

The outfield player has more time to set up and prepare himself for oncoming balls, as compared to an infielder. It is important that he fields the ball cleanly, or at least keeps it in front of his body. If the ball gets by him, it could lead to the batter advancing to another base or even scoring a run.

● Stand with your feet apart and knees bent. Be ready to react as soon as the ball is hit.

● Get your body behind the ball, and then kneel down on your throwing side, with your glove covering the gap between your legs.

● Position your body at about 45 degrees to the ball. This will help you block the ball should it take a bad bounce.

ready position ▶ ▶ field the ball ▶

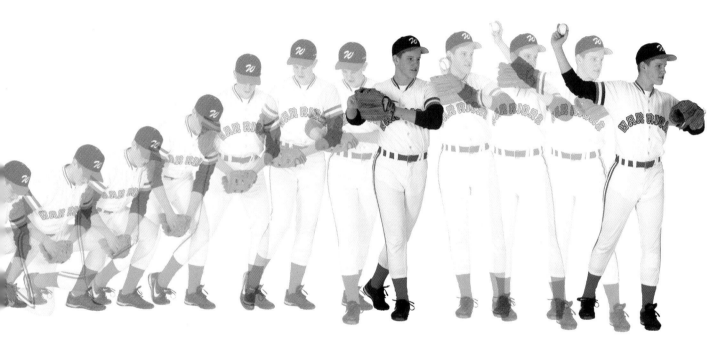

● Try to field the ball cleanly with two hands. If you can't, block the ball with your body to keep it in front of you.

● As you straighten up, transfer the ball to your right hand, and step forward with your right leg as you prepare to throw.

● Bring the ball above your ear and point your glove toward your target. As you start to throw, step toward your target with your left leg.

● Aim at the chest of the fielder you are throwing to and follow through as you release the ball. Note that you can use the crow hop here to gain more power (see page 68).

▶ **stand up** ▶ ▶ **throw** ■

fielding

catching a fly ball and crow hop

The most important thing to remember when catching a fly ball is to use two hands. The crow hop includes a normal throwing action, but the added hop gives the outfielder more power to throw the ball a greater distance.

● Stand with your feet apart and knees bent. Outfielders should always know where to throw the ball when it is hit to them.

● To get a good jump on the ball, it is best to move laterally first, using a crossover step. If you automatically run in as a fly ball is hit to you, you will find many of them going over your head.

● Position yourself under the flight of the ball. Stretch your hands up slightly to your throwing side, with your glove at about 45 degrees and your right hand beside it.

● As you catch the ball, close the glove with your right hand to stop the ball from popping out. Allow your hands to "give" with the ball.

● Once you have caught the ball, step forward onto your right foot, turned at 45 degrees. Take a short hop on your right foot to give your body forward momentum.

● As you do so, transfer the ball to your throwing hand, and turn your body side on. As you land on your right foot, bring your throwing hand up above your ear and step forward with your left foot.

● As this is a long throw, extend your arm fully and throw "over the top." Follow through fully to gain maximum distance.

drop step

The drop step is used to run back to catch a ball that has been hit over your head. It stops you from running backward on your heels and helps you get to the ball as quickly as possible.

● Stand with your feet apart on the balls of your feet, knees bent, and ready to react to the ball once it is hit.

● As the ball is hit, take a "drop" step backward in the direction that the ball is traveling.

● Pivot on your back foot and start to run as quickly as possible toward where you think the ball will land.

● As you run, keep your eye on the ball by looking over your shoulder. Always run on your toes, not on your heels.

● Raise your glove early so you can make any minor adjustments needed to catch the ball at the last moment.

● Once you have caught the ball, turn back to face the infield, ready to throw to another fielder if necessary.

● Note: this is one of the few plays where you may have to catch a fly ball using only one hand.

▶ **raise glove early** ▶ **catch the ball** ▶ **turn to infield** ■

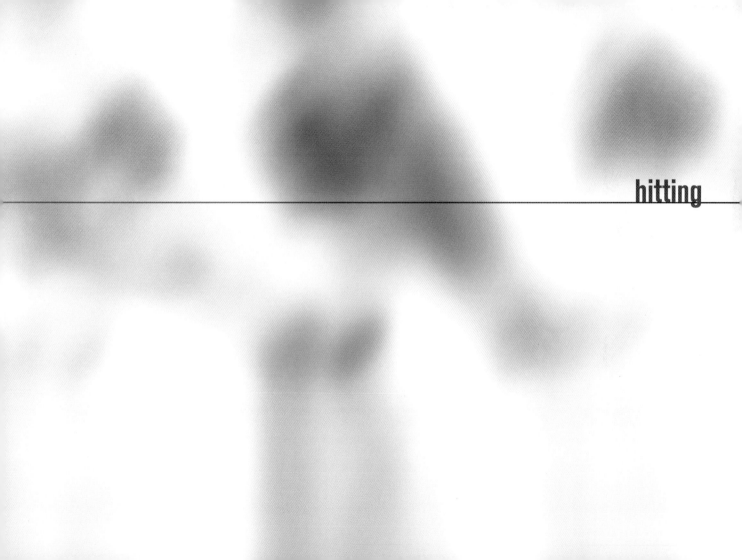

hitting

the swing

There are many different styles of hitting, but all share the same fundamental principles. The idea is to find a style that is comfortable for you. To judge what distance you should be standing from home plate, reach down and touch the far edge of the plate with the tip of your bat.

● Stand side on to the pitcher with your feet roughly shoulder width apart, knees slightly bent, hands around shoulder height and slightly away from the body. This should be a relaxed and comfortable position.

● As the pitcher is about to deliver the pitch, transfer most of your weight to your back (right) leg and move your hands slightly away from the pitcher. This is known as loading.

● As the ball is pitched, step directly toward the pitcher, landing on the ball of your left (front) foot. Keep your weight and your hands back.

● Begin to turn your hips toward the pitcher while pivoting on the ball of your back foot. As you turn your hips, start to move your hands straight toward the pitcher. Keep your swing as level as possible.

● At the point of contact, your arms should be extended, left leg straight or slightly bent; right leg slightly bent; body straight; the fingernails of your right hand facing up; weight evenly balanced; head in; and eyes on the ball.

● After the bat makes contact with the ball, your wrists should roll over, allowing the follow-through to begin.

● Finish with a smooth follow-through. Your chin should start the swing on your left shoulder and finish on your right. This will help you keep your eye on the ball and your head in.

▶ **make contact** ▶ **roll wrists** ▶ **follow through**

sacrifice bunt

hitting

This advances a runner by allowing yourself to be put out at first base. The bat should start level with the top of the strike zone for two reasons: 1) any pitch above your bat will be out of the strike zone (you only want to bunt strikes); 2) if you start your bat low in the strike zone and come up to meet a pitch higher in the zone, you are likely to pop the ball up and be caught out.

● Start in your normal batting position because you don't want the opposition to know you are going to bunt the ball.

● Take a short step forward on your left (front) leg, turning to face the pitcher. Pivot on your right (back) foot through 90 degrees.

● Slide your right (top) hand up a third of the length of the bat, holding it pinched between your thumb and index finger to protect your hand.

■   normal stance   ▶   square around   ▶   adjust your grip   ▶

● Now bend your knees and extend your arms, keeping your elbows slightly bent and relaxed. Hold the bat level, or at an angle with the bat head slightly raised.

● Watch the ball all the way onto the bat. Do not try to hit the ball. Instead, let the ball hit the bat. Let your arms "give," to absorb the impact of the pitch.

● Try to meet the ball squarely on the bat. Do not get underneath the ball as this may pop the ball up in the air and it could be caught. If the ball is caught the base runner could be "doubled off" too (see page 13).

● The idea is to knock the ball down on the ground about 10 to 20 feet along either baseline. This will make it hard to field and impossible to get the runner out at second base.

bend your knees ▶ **let ball hit bat** ▶ **get ball down** ■

bunt for a base hit—right hand

The purpose of a bunt for a base hit is to reach first base safely. The key to doing this successfully is the element of surprise—making the opposition think you are batting normally until the last possible moment.

● Start in your normal batting position because you do not want the opposition to know you are planning to bunt the ball.

● Drop your right foot back behind your left, ready to run to first base. At the same time, begin to move your top (right) hand up the bat.

● Slide your right hand up a third of the length of the bat, holding it pinched between your thumb and index finger to protect your hand.

● Do not extend your arms, but keep your bottom (left) hand close to your left hip so you can leave it until the last minute to bring your bat around to bunt the ball. Angle the bat toward third base.

● Watch the ball all the way onto the bat. Do not try to hit the ball. Instead, let the ball hit the bat. Try to bunt the ball 10 to 20 feet along the third baseline.

● Make sure the ball is down before you start to run. As soon as you have hit the ball, drop the bat by your side and run to first base.

● Do not tread on the plate or step out of the batter's box as you bunt the ball or you will be called out.

angle bat to third base ▶ **let ball hit bat** ▶ **drop the bat and run** ▶ ■

bunt for a base hit—left hand

It is easier for a left-hander to bunt for a base hit as he can start running toward first base as he bunts the ball. However, he must be careful not to step out of the batter's box before he makes contact with the ball, or he will be called out.

● Start in your normal batting position because you do not want the opposition to know you are planning to bunt the ball.

● Turn your front (right) foot toward the pitcher, then turn your body and transfer your weight on to your right foot.

● As you do so, slide your top (left) hand up a third of the length of the bat, holding it pinched between your thumb and index finger to protect your hand.

● Do not extend your arms but bring your bottom (right) hand in front of your left hip so you can leave it to the last minute to bring your bat around to bunt the ball. Angle the bat toward third base.

● At the same time, begin to step toward first base. Watch the ball all the way onto the bat. Do not try to hit the ball, but let the ball hit the bat instead.

● With the bat facing toward third base, try to bunt the ball 10 to 20 feet along the third baseline.

● Get the ball down as you start to run. Drop the bat and run toward first base as quickly as possible.

▶ make contact ▶ start running ▶ run to first base ■

base running

primary and secondary lead

The idea of a primary and secondary lead is to get you nearer to second base, but close enough to return to first base should the pitcher or catcher attempt a pick-off. Keep your eye on the pitcher at all times. **(This sequence runs from right to left.)**

● After the third sidestep, maintain an even balance and be ready to run toward second base or break back toward first base, depending on the result of the pitch.

● Sidestep to your right three times. Keep your hands out in front of you to help with your balance and watch to see what happens to the pitch.

● When the pitcher has committed himself to pitch to the batter, start to take your secondary lead.

● Keep watching the pitcher at all times and maintain a low center of gravity, as you may need to dive back to first base at any moment.

● Take two-and-a-half of these steps in total. This is your primary lead. Do not cross your legs at any time, and watch the pitcher closely.

● Take a sideways step with your right foot, and drag your left foot toward your right. Your feet should be wide apart, with knees bent and your hands loose in front of you for balance.

● Start with your left foot on first base, and look toward your third base coach for a signal. Do not leave the base until the pitcher has made contact with the rubber.

stay low to the ground   ◄   **primary lead**   ◄   **take sideways step**   ◄   **look for sign**   ■

stealing second base

This is an aggressive move by the base runner to advance to second base without the ball being hit. Speed and reading the pitcher well are essential. Take your normal primary lead and be ready to run once the pitcher begins to throw to the batter **(This sequence runs from right to left.)**

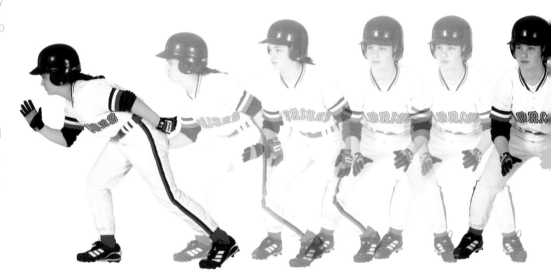

● The primary lead usually consists of two-and-a-half steps, but you can vary it depending on the pitcher's pick-off moves and your aggressiveness as a base runner.

● As soon as the pitcher commits himself to pitch to the batter, pivot on your right foot. Bring your left foot across and run to second base. Remain low as you take your first few steps.

● Once you have your primary lead, watch the pitcher closely to enable you to get a good jump.

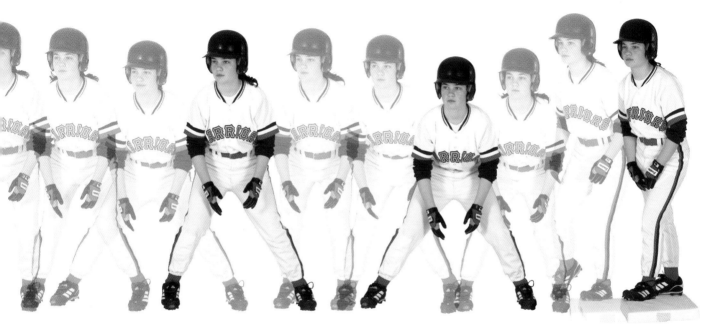

● Keep your body low throughout. Be ready to return to first base if the pitcher decides to try to pick you off.

● Remember to make sideways steps, sliding your left foot to your right foot without crossing your legs.

● Once you have received the signal, begin to take your primary lead. As described as page 85, watch the pitcher closely at all times.

● Once you have safely reached first base, place your left foot on the base and look for a signal from the third-base coach.

returning to first base on a pick-off

By being prepared to dive back to first base when the pitcher
attempts a pick-off, you can afford to take a longer lead.

● Once you have taken your primary
lead, maintain a low center of gravity
and stay on the balls of your feet,
ready to return to first base should
the pitcher attempt a pick-off.

● As soon as you see the pitcher
start his pick-off move, pivot on your
right foot, staying low and leaning
toward first base.

● At the same time, push off your
right foot as you start to dive toward
first base. Focus on the outside corner
of the base.

● Do not dive through the air, but
"drop and drive" yourself along the
ground instead, staying as low as
possible.

● Keep your head down and your body low. Allow your momentum to carry you toward the base.

● Stretch your right arm out so your hand reaches toward the outside corner of first base.

● By reaching out with your right hand, you offer the first baseman the least amount of your body to tag.

● Once you have safely returned to first base, stand up, keeping in contact with the base *at all times* until the ball has been returned to the pitcher.

basic slide *running*

The two reasons for sliding into a base are to prevent you from overrunning the base and from being tagged out. This sequence describes leading with your left leg. If you prefer to lead with your right, substitute right for left.

● As you are running, focus on the base and prepare to start your slide about 8 to 10 feet from it.

● Stretch your front (left) leg out toward the base. At the same time, begin to lean your body backward.

● Launch yourself toward the base off your back (right) leg and aim to land on your right buttock. Do not leap up high into the air. Instead, keep your body relaxed as you let it fall to the ground.

● As you start to slide, extend your left leg out in front of you, keeping it slightly bent and relaxed. Keep both arms out in front of you.

● Bend your right knee so that your right foot is under the knee of your left leg. Reach up with your arms.

● As you slide along the ground, allow your body and arms to fall backward, behind your head. Keep your body as low to the ground as possible.

● You should be reaching out toward the base with your left foot at about a 45-degree angle. This will help to avoid injury to the fielder if you hit him with your cleats.

● As your left foot hits the edge of the base, allow your left knee to bend to absorb the force of the impact. Your body should now be lying flat on the ground

begin slide ▶ **keep low** ▶ **reach out with right foot** ▶ **lie flat**

hook slide *running*

This is a more difficult slide, but can be a very effective way to avoid being tagged out. This is because most of your body is away from the base and the fielder will have more difficulty reaching you.

● As you are running, focus on the base and prepare to start your slide about 8 to 10 feet from it.

● Lean your body backward as you stretch your left leg out to the side. Start to move your arms forward and upward.

● Hold your hands out in front of you for balance as you launch off your right foot. Do not leap into the air, but allow your body to fall to the ground, with your legs apart.

● Let your body fall to the left so you land on your left buttock. Reach out for the corner of the base with your right foot.

● Allow your body and arms to fall back over your head. Your whole body except your arms should be in contact with the ground as you slide.

● As your right foot makes contact with the corner of the base, let your right knee bend to absorb the force of the impact.

● Do not jump into the hook slide because you risk injuring yourself and you will also reduce the speed and effectiveness of your slide.

index

B

backhanding a ball 50–51
backstop 8
ball (equipment) 9
  basic catching 20–21
  grip 18, 24
  pitching 24–35
  throwing 18–19
balls (pitch) 6, 7
base hit 7
  bunt for 78–81
base running 13–14, 84–93
  forced 14
  hook slide 92–93
  primary lead 84–85
  returning to first base 88–89
  secondary lead 84–85
  slides 14, 90–93
  stealing 10, 12, 14, 28–29
  stealing second base 86–87
  tagging 14, 54–55
  unforced 14
base umpire 7
bases 8
  tagging runners 54–55
  see also base running; first base;
  second base; third base
basic catching 20–21
basic slide 90–91
basic swing 74–75
basic throwing 18–19

bats 9, 11
batters
  gloves 9
  hitting 11–12, 74–81
  out/safe 7
  strikes/balls 6
batter's box 8
blocking home plate 42–43
breaking pitches 10
bunt 12
  for a base hit 78–81
  sacrifice fly 12, 76–77

C

catcher 12, 38–45
  blocking home plate 12, 42–43
  blocking wild pitches 12, 38–39
  catcher's box 8
  catching pop-ups 12, 44–45
  mitt 9
  tagging 13, 14
  throwing to second base 40–41
catcher's box 8
catching 12, 38–45
  backhanding a ball 50–51
  basic 20–21
  double play pivot 60–63
  drop step 70–71
  first baseman stretch 56–57
  fly balls 68–69
  relay 64–65
  tagging runners 54–55
center fielder 8, 13
change-up 10, 11
coaches 7

crossover step 52–53
  backhanding a ball 50–51
  fly balls 68
crow hop 68–69

D

diving, returning to first base 88–89
double play 13
  feed 58–59
  pivot 60–63
double play pivot
  second baseman 62–63
  short stop 60–61
drop step 70–71

E

equipment 9

F

fair balls 7
fair territory 8
fastball 10, 11
feed, double play 58–59
fence 8
fielding 13, 48–71
  backhanding a ball 50–51
  crossover step 52–53
  double play 58–63
  first baseman stretch 56–57
  gloves 9
  ground balls 48–49, 66–67
  relay 64–65
  tagging runners 54–55
  see also infielders; outfielders
fielding position

set position 29, 31
windup 25, 27
first base
  pick-off to 32–35
  primary lead 84–85
  returning to 88–89
  secondary lead 84–85
first baseman 8, 13
  mitt 9
  stretch 56–57
fly balls
  catching 68–69
  sacrifice fly 12
fly out 7
forced running 14

foul balls 7
    base running 14
    catching pop-ups 44–45
    strikes 6
foul lines 8
foul territory 8

G

gloves 9
    backhanding a ball 50–51
    basic catching 20–21
    blocking wild pitches 38–39
    catching fly balls 68–69
    catching pop-ups 45
    crossover step 52–53
    double play feed 58–59
    double play pivot 60–61, 62
    drop step 71
    fielding a ground ball 48
    first baseman stretch 57
    relay 64
    set position 28–31
    tagging runners 54–55
    throwing 18
    throwing to second base 40–41
    windup 24–27
ground balls
    fielding 48–49, 66–67
    hit and run 12
ground out 7

H

helmets 9
hit and run 12
hitting 11–12, 74–81

the swing 74–75
bunt for a base hit 78–81
sacrifice bunt 76–77
home plate 8
    blocking 12, 42–43
    distance from when batting 74
hook slide 14, 92–93

I

infield 8
    ground balls 48–49
infielders 13
    gloves 9
    see also first baseman; second
    baseman; shortstop; third
    baseman

L

leading off 14
    see also primary lead; secondary
    lead
left fielder 8, 13
left hand
    bunt for a base hit 80–81
    pick-off to first base 34–35
    set position 30–31
    windup 26–27
loading, basic swing 74

M

managers 7
masks
    blocking home plate 42–43
    catching pop-ups 44–45
mitts see gloves

O

out 7, 13
outfield 7, 8, 12, 13
outfielders 13
    fly balls 68–69
    ground balls 66–67
    see also center fielder; left fielder;
    right fielder

P

pick-off to first base
    left hand 34–35
    right hand 32–33
pick-offs
    returning to first base 88–89
    to first base 32–35
pitcher 8, 10–11, 24–35
    catcher 12
pitcher's mound 8
pitcher's plate 8
    windup 24
pitching 10–11, 24–35
    balls 6
    mixing 11
    pick-off to first base 32–35
    set position 28–31
    strikes 6
    windup 24–27
pivot, double play 60–63
plate umpire 7
pop-up slide 14
pop-ups, catching 12, 44–45
primary lead 84–85
    returning to first base 88–89
    stealing second base 86–87

R

relay 64–65
right fielder 8, 13
right hand
    bunt for a base hit 78–79
    pick-off to first base 32–33
    set position 28–29
    windup 24–25
runners on base
    blocking wild pitches 12, 38–39
    throwing to second base 40–41

S

sacrifice bunt 12, 76–77
sacrifice fly 12
safe 7
safety 9
scorers 7
second base
    double play 58–59
    stealing 86–87
second baseman 8
    double play pivot 62–63
secondary lead 84–85
set position 10
    left hand 30–31
    pick-off to first base 32
    right hand 28–29
shortstop 8, 13
    double play pivot 60–61
signals
    catcher 12
    pitching 24
single 7
slides 14

basic 90–91
blocking home plate 42–43
hook slide 92–93
returning to first base 88–89
tagging runners 54–55
squeeze 12
stealing 14
   pitches 10
   second base 86–87
   set position 28–29
stretch (fielding), first baseman 56–57

stretch (pitch) see set position
stretches (warming up) 9
strike out 6, 7
strike zone 6, 11–12
strikes 6, 7

T
tag out 7
   blocking home plate 43
   catcher 12
tagging 54–55
   catcher 12

pick-off to first base 32–35
throwing to second base 40–41
tagging-up 14
third baseman 8
throwing
   backhanding a ball 51
   basic 18–19
   crossover step 53
   crow hop 69
   double play feed 59
   double play pivot 60–61, 63
   fielding ground balls 67

ground balls 49
pick-off to first base 33, 35
relay 64–65
to second base 40–41
see also pitching
throwing to second base, catchers 40–41

U
umpires 7
unforced running 14

W
walks 6, 7
warming up 9
wild pitches, catcher 12, 38–39
windup 10
   left hand 26–27
   right hand 24–25